SMLuke

# VIGILANTES RIDE IN 1882

*Oldie Neil is dead . . . dead through these long lonely years, he sleeps on a low hill north of Rockford, oblivious to wars, to the arrogance of men in high station. He does not hear the drone of jet aircraft in the blue sky overhead or the thunder of diesel Caterpillars climbing Palouse hills, he lies so quietly in the cool earth in eastern Washington . . . and no shy but determined girls will quietly unbutton soft white blouses for Oldie Neil . . . who sleeps so peacefully . . .*

This is his story . . .

# Vigilantes Ride in 1882

Herbert Stevens

Ye Galleon Press
Fairfield, Washington
1994

**Library of Congress Cataloging in Publication Data**

Stevens, Herbert, 1892-

Vigilantes ride in 1882.

1. Lynching--Washington--Case studies.
2. Neil, Oldie, d. 1882. 3. Vigilance committees--
Washington Territory, I. Title.
HV6469 1882.S73 364.1'34 75-38603
ISBN 0-87770-148-2

# HERBERT STEVENS

*On summer evenings the ghost of Oldie Neil floats gently, softly up and down the winding curves of the South Fork of Rock Creek . . . and on winter nights it moans through the pine trees high up on Plummer Mountain . . . . .*

This is the story of the lynching of a purportedly innocent 19 year old boy named *Oldie Neil*, who was hanged in Rock Creek Valley in the early summer of 1882, by a citizen's committee, for the alleged crime of stealing horses.

The locale of the events that I shall try to chronicle is a fertile valley, extending from the town of Rockford, south and east for a distance of about ten miles. It extends over into Idaho and is known as Rock Creek Valley.

Rock Creek is the principal tributary of the historic Hangman Creek, and was known to the Indians as *Naquilpha*. It takes its name from the extremely rocky canyon that establishes its course from the town of Rockford to the confluence with Hangman Creek at the little settlement of Duncan.

From Rockford south and east to its source the valley broadens and branches into a fertile farming country. It has its source or sources in four separate branches, known locally as the East Fork, heading near Worley, Idaho; the Middle Fork, heading in the mountains west of Worley; the South Fork that heads in the extreme southwest corner of Kootenai County, Idaho; and Mica Creek from the foot of Mica Peak, that is really a tributary instead of a branch.

The portion of the Valley that is drained by the South Fork above where it is joined by the Middle Fork was known as the upper Valley, and the part below this junction and east was known as the Lower Valley.

# HERBERT STEVENS

Rock Creek at that time ran full of water the year around. The settlers kept row boats and good sized salmon were taken in the spring. Today, due to cutting off the timber and plowing up of the prairie sod, it is dry, except in wet season of the year or in case of an occasional extra heavy rain.

The first settler in the valley was A. L. Bradley who came in the spring of 1877 and settled where the East Fork flows into the South Fork, about two miles east of where the town of Rockford was soon to appear. The farm is now the home of Mr. and Mrs. Orin Lee. Mr. Bradley was followed before fall by Charles F. Hecht, Martin McCoy, and the next year, 1878, by Alex La Shaw, all of whom settled adjoining or near.

According to Jonathan Edwards in *A History of Spokane County*, published in 1900, "Bradley spent the first winter without seeing a human face"—this I doubt, for he had the afore mentioned neighbors and the Indians.

The following spring (1878) a saw mill was built on Mica Flat just before it empties into Rock Creek, and the town of Rockford had its beginnings. The origin of the name is obvious. The mill was built by A. N. Worley and his cousin, Clint Farnsworth, who were Rockford's co-founders. The machinery for the mill was all freighted up by teams from Walla Walla, which was the closest settlement at that time. The mill, by providing lumber, was an important factor in the rapid growth of the new settlement of Rockford, and according to C. A. Worley, a brother of A. N. Worley, who joined his brother in 1880, "by the spring of 1882 there were at least a dozen families or fifty souls who considered the new town their permanent home."

# VIGILANTES RIDE IN 1882

In the spring of 1882 the Upper Valley was settled by another group of about a dozen families, who were refugees from the Modoc War in Oregon. They were the usual hard working, God fearing, hardy breed of pioneer, that settled much of the Pacific Northwest. Most of them had come north from California by covered wagon.

Their first act after establishing themselves in their meager homes was to organize and build a church. This they called the Rockford Bethel Methodist Church, and I believe was the first Methodist church to be built north of the Snake River. It was the parent of the present Methodist Church of Rockford. It was located a short distance to your right (north) of the highway as you travel from Plummer, Idaho, to Fairfield, and is one and one-quarter miles west of the Washington-Idaho state line. It was near the old Alpine School and it stood until about fifty years ago when it was torn down and the material used in the construction of a barn on the Charles Hecht, Jr. farm, located a little way east of Rockford. The church was the property of its successor, the Rockford Methodist Church. The church building was sold to Mr. Hecht, a member of the congregation of the Rockford Methodist Church, who took the building down about 1923.

The first paster of the Rockford Bethel Methodist Church was a man of group named Ed Henderson, and it was said that he shed much of his ministerial dignity and some of his piety, upon descending from the pulpit.

From here the story as told by several surviving old timers that I have talked to, has several versions, differing in some details but agreeing in many ways. It is certain that there would be no way of anyone but a participant knowing the truth, and there would be even less chance to verify the truth after the passage of so much time, even if it had ever been public knowledge, which it was not, ( to lift a thought from Father Stanley, an authority and author of pioneer history) —"The passage of time incorporates and accepts legend as truth, and certainly more un-truth is accepted as true, than are facts."

Certainly much must be accepted as born of fertile imagination and no doubt much is colored by exaggeration. I believe that a combination of the stories as told by C. A. Worley and Jess Gilbert—each past 92 years of age and each living in the community in 1882, and each still living here, should be as nearly correct as it would be possible to ascertain now. Mr. Worley knew Oldie Neil and had talked to him the day before he was lynched, and saw the body hanging from the tree. Mr. Gilbert was a member of the congregation of the Bethel Church, that acted as a Citizen's Committee and according to his own account was not a member of the lynching party—"because one of my daughters was very sick and my wife begged me not to leave." Their versions vary slightly but agree on essentials, and they should have been in a position to be correct on the details that they supply.

The popular version, as near as I have been able to gather it, is more fantastic and I should give it first and note some changes that I believe to more nearly correct later. According to the story as met with most often: Among the settlers in the Upper Valley, that had just moved in from Oregon, were two brothers, of very different mien. One of them was industrious and respected and was liked by all who knew him. He numbered among the members of his household three orphaned children of his wife's deceased sister. They were two teen aged sisters and their older brother,

Oldie, who was nineteen. This boy was soon to become the unenviable hero of this story.

The other of these two brothers is described as the exact opposite. He is said to have been a burly brutal bully, who wore a red beard trimmed square at the bottom and foot long. He is said to have been of a 'mean countenance and a shifty eye.' He was disliked, distrusted and feared by all. Because of his red beard he was known as 'Red.' Red was suspected and no doubt rightfully of being a member of an organized band of horse thieves that operated a string of stations from their old homes in Oregon to the Canadian border. Their racket being to steal horses in the north and drive them south as replacements for horses that they stole in the south to drive north, ad infinitum, in a vicious circle of near perpetual motion. It was a lucrative practice, not accepted or approved of by respectable citizens.

Thus he had accumulated a valuable band of horses that he hired his brother's orphaned nephew to herd for him. And these Oldie cared for and pastured on the fertile hills near where the Plummer-Fairfield highway crosses the state line. Here he had built a sturdy one room log cabin and pole corral and claimed the adjoining land by 'squatter's rights.'

It is almost certain that Red and his gang never stole stock from the community in which he lived—but his reputation was not good, and when a man who lived near the junction of the Middle and South Fork missed horses from his pasture, Red was immediately suspected. It was later learned that these horses had strayed and were not stolen. At the immediate time no one knew this and no one stopped to consider the possibility. This loss acted as a last straw in arousing the community to action.

At the time a series of old-fashioned revival meetings were being held at the Bethel Church, and on a Sunday morning in June of 1882, the men of the congregation met after church services to consider Red's nefarious ways and decide upon a 'cure' for them. This extempore vigilante meeting behaved as most such meetings do, and as usual, was inspired by the urging of a self appointed leader known because of his 'eleoquence' as the Judge.

At this trial Red was tried, judged, and found guilty and sentenced to be hanged for horse stealing, all without one defense or protest. And as usual he was not asked to be present to explain. The defendent at such trials was seldom present for obvious reasons. One would be that they would not wish to be so readily available to the committee appoint to effect the punishment. Immediately after the 'trial' a posse of seven of the bolder men of the committee left at once to execute the demands of the sentence. Red was soon apprehended and by way of saving his own neck (figuratively as well as literally) he denied his own guilt and implicated Oldie as the guilty party. The posse accepted this with no question and set out at once in quest of Oldie, leaving Red free to make his get away, which he did without delay.

It seems strange that the posse could have been so easily diverted and stranger yet that they would so easily have accepted the word of one whom, by their own actions they distrusted to the point of having within the hour, condemned to death as a horse thief. It is also strange that even their brand of 'justice' would not have suggested a new trial for a new suspect.

The posse that was soon to become a lynching party went at once to Oldie's cabin where they arrived early in the afternoon. Oldie was apprehensive because of their sinister appearance and probably by a knowledge that the horses were stolen, had barricaded himself behind the thick walls of his cabin. It is said that several volleys were fired into the walls of the little 'fort' and it was the thick walls of this 'fort' that prolonged his life for a worse fate. As the excitement of the battle wore off, a parley was held, through the walls of the cabin. It was said that Oldie denied stealing the horses, but admitted that he knew they were dishonestly acquired by his uncle 'Red.' It was agreed that in exchange for voluntary surrender he would be guaranteed safe conduct to, and a fair trial, at the then one year old Spokane County Seat at Cheney. In exchange for this promise it is said that he gave himself into the hands of the posse made up of men whose word he accepted as respected neighbors and friends.

There were seven men up to this point. Five of them left at once with their prisoner, in a three seated hack, or buckboard, supposedly for Cheney, while the other two returned to the church to report to those who awaited them there. It is evident that there had been no intent to keep the promise of safe conduct to Cheney, for they hardly started in that direction, but proceeded in almost the opposite direction. They went without deliberation or hesitation nearly ten miles almost due north to within about two miles of Rockford, where the lynching took place.

The two men who had returned to the church led back a second party to intercept the first party and stage a faked attack and holdup on the prisoner and his custodians. This they did, and this surely must have been by prearrangement. The second party cut in ahead of the first party and intercepted them at the junction of the South Fork and the East Fork, in what is known as Hecht's Grove, and here the lynching took place. This is about at the intersection of the old Rockford-Worley highway, with the new highway between those towns. The hangman's tree stood but a few yards south of the new concrete bridge, and within the angle formed by the junction of the two roads.

Late in the evening of that long June Sunday, the Hechts, who lived a quarter of a mile away, were startled by a volley of shots from the woods a short distance down the creek from their home. This was answered almost immediately by a stronger barrage from the other side of the creek. They thought the gun-fire strange, in fact they were apprehensive of their own safety and took precautions to defend themselves, and remained on guard the rest of the night.

Early the next morning two neighbors, Dave Vess and Martin McCoy, brought them the news of a dead man hanging from a tree beside the road, in their pasture.

Investigation indentified the dead man as Oldie Neil, a boy from the Upper Valley who had worked for Mr. Hecht, and whom Mrs. Hecht long years later, remembered as having been "industrious, pleasant and likeable." Charley Feeley, a pioneer of Rathdrum Prairie, who was then a small boy living with his parents and A. L. Bradley, remembers the excitement of that day.

The body could not be moved until after the sheriff and coronor had been called and had made their investigation. A messenger was sent on horse back to Cheney and the two officials arrived by the same mode of travel on the following day. The body was taken down on the second day and buried on the hill across Mica Creek from where the town stood. The grave is said to be near the residence accupied by George Robinson, and later by a Mr. Hoisington.

# VIGILANTES RIDE IN 1882

Oldie's two sisters had come to the Hecht home in the meantime but were restrained from visiting the scene of the crime. Upon hearing of Uncle Sylas's cowardly perfidy it is said they swore theyh would avenge their brother's death.

After the hanging all hands had returned to their homes in the Upper Valley where they told a wild story of having been attacked by a larger group of armed men, of having defended their prisoner with their last shot, and of having been over powered and having their prisoner taken from them, and of seeing him hanged from a tree. This story sounded fanatastic in some ways and found little credence with the public

In the first place the families of Bradly, Feeley and Hecht all lived almost within shouting distance and at least four more families lived a little more than a mile distant and the village of Rockford was only two miles away, yet they rode ten miles to their homes without making a report or an appeal for help. Nor in all the exchange of shots had anyone received a scratch or a bruise, and no attempt was made to apprehend or punish those guilty of this sordid affair.

It was evident that as he fate became evident Oldie had made a violent struggle. When found his hands and feet were bound and his body bore evidence of having been brutally handled. The rig in which he had been transported had been driven but a few yards off the main traveled wagon trail, to beneath a low limb traveling from a scrubby pine tree, where a rope had been looped around his neck and the other end made fast to the limb and tthe wagon driven from under him. It is said that a little more than a foot of space cleared his feet from the ground.

# HERBERT STEVENS

Several things are hard to account for, one is the reason for making a ten mile trip from the place of his capture to the scene of his hanging. Perhaps they thought the removing the scene of the crime from their end of the valley would remove suspicion of guilt from them. Some think it was done to point the finger of suspicion towards the neighbors of the Lower Valley.

There was very little doubt as to the identity of those implicated in the crime, but no charges were ever brought and no attempt seems to have been made to do so.

Tradition has it that every one of the principals in this lynching suffered a horrible end, by murder, by accident, or by loss of sanity. The Judge it is said moved to the Big Bend where he and his wife were burned to death in a fire that destroyed their home. Red was found almost completely decapitated by an unknown asssilant in Stevens County.

One man was killed inhis own field by being run over with a disk harrow hitched behind his run-away four horse team. One is aid to have become delerious in sickness and was allowed no company during his last lingering illnes. These stories may be more fiction than truth—I have not tried to credit or discredit them. Even the tree suffered the traditional ill lot of a hangman's tree. It was a lone, scrubby forked pine, with a taller pine for a companion. Lightning struck and killed the taller pine and after several years someone set a fire that burned the dead 'snag'. Its burning trunk fell into the fork of the hangman's tree and both of them crashed to the ground, carrying out the old superstition that a tree never thrives after having borne such gruesome fruit. After lying on the ground for some years Vern Hecht and his father cut up what remained of the trunk of the tree for firewood, this about 1931.

As an anticlimax, in a lighter mood, a few days after the lynching, an ancient woman of the Coeur d'Alene tribe came to town wearing Oldie's old cap. It had been lost and overlooked in the excitement of his struggles with his captors. The old woman had found the cap along the trail as she trudged her way to town, and had accepted it as a gift from Heaven, nor could she be induced to give it up. It became a permanet addition to her Sunday apparel for as long as she appeared on the streets of Rockford. A slightly different version is told by Mr. Charles O. Worley, who was born in 1860 ana wno came to Rockford in 1880 and has lived in or near the town ever since. He was for many years Agent for the Coeur d'Alene Indians, and it was him that the town of Worley, Idaho, was named. Mr. Worley was 92 years of age when he was interviewed by the author, and the case of Oldie Neil discussed in detail.

Mr. Worley gives Oldie a father and two sisters all living in the Upper Valley, and makes the Judge Oldie's uncle who betrayed him. He has the Judge move to Springdale, in Stevens County, where he was found in June of 1892, shot to death by unknown hands and his body dumped into the mire of the not too sanitary hog pen. Mr. Worley had been slightly hurt at his work in his brother's saw mill and was not working on the Monday morning that Oldie's body was discovered. He gives this account: 'A man named Justin drove by on the running gears of his wagon and asked me, did you ever see a dead man hanging from a tree? Well, climb on, I'm going to see one. When we got there I recognized Oldie Neil, and his father and two sisters were sitting on a log at one side of the road. Oldie's cap was on the log between them. I got close enough to recognize Oldie and I said to Justin, "I've seen enough," and I turned around and walked back to town.

Mr. Worley is absolutely certain that but two men escorted Oldie to his death ride from the scene of his capture to that of his execution. He heard them admit the next day that they did so, and that they drove immediately to Cheney and reported that they had been attacked and forced to give up their prisoner by a masked mob. This puts a slightly different face on the affair but it does not disprove collusion between them and the mob.

The sheriff's name was Mike Hawthorne and he made quite a pretense of investigation, then returned to Cheney, and dropped all interest in the case.

Mr. Worley describes Oldie Neil as having been of "of good deportment and a pleasant companion."

Mr. J. P. Gilbert, also 92 years of age in 1952, when interviewed by the author, and a first settler in the Upper Valley, and still a resident of the community, gives a similar account. He says they were holding revival meetings in the Bethel Church and that Edd Henderson, a layman, was their pastor. He makes the Judge a confidant of the man who stole the horses. He gives Oldie an older brother and a brother-in-law, and says the boys stayed at the Judge's home and according to Mr. Gilbert it was the Judge who implicated the boys in order to vindicate himself and his confederates in crime. He says that the arrest of the two boys was attempted in the Judge's home and that the other two made their escape.

The *Rockford Enterprise* was established in 1885 in Rockford and the editorship soon devolved on Mr. Henry Desgranges, then still in his teens, and preumably the youngest editor ever to publish a newspaper in Washington Territory, or state. It has been rumored that in the 1880's or 1890's that this newspaper under editor Desgranges, published an anonymous confession by one of the members of the lynching party, with promise of more installments later. I have tried to find a copy of this particular issue without success, and have tried to locate someone who might have read this article, and who could remember the details. Now I know why I have not succeded in this effort. Last Memorial Day I had the pleasure and honor of meeting and talking with Mr. Desgranges, now living in Kennewick, Washington, and he tells me that such a confession never was published.

It is also said that there are deathbed confessions from three members of the lynching party on file in the Spokane County Sheriff's office. This I have never tried to verify, for I do not believe they exist.

Mr Gilbert gives Oldie an older brother, Jess, and a brother-in-law named McEwan. He has three boys staying with the Judge. He says Jess and McEwan escaped and Oldie was taken from a log cabin used as a bunk house and that was later used as a hog house by a later owner, Charles Holsten. Lyman Holsten, well known in Fairfield and Rockford was raised on this farm and has heard old timers tell that a man was arrested in the old log house house and hanged near Rockford. The remains of the old log cabin from which Oldie was taken were destroyed about 1915.

The Judge's home was perhaps a mile nearly due south from the church on land now owend by Orland Ostheller. Old timers say he log cabin and corral stood until about 1915. Mr. Gilbert says that the Judge moved farther south to near Latah, where he and his wife were later found shot to death by unknown hands.

Neither Mr. Worley nor Mr. Gilbert will admit that Red Sylas ever existed, but to some he seems to have been very real.

After about fifteen years a quiet, taciturn man claiming to be Oldie's older brother, appeared in Rockford and made some inquiries and vanished as quietly as he had come. He was never seen or heard of again in the community. It would complete my story could his visit be coupled to the death of Red Sylas, if he existed, or that of the Judge if Red is imaginary, but I must admit this is only a quirk of my own fancy for I have neither the coincident of time or place upon which to base such workings of my own imagination.

Neither Mr. Worley or Mr. Gilbert will admit there ever was a Red Sylas, however Red Sylas seems very real to Cobe Smally who was a boy of ten at the time. I am inclined to put greater credence in the versions of Mr. Worley and Mr. Gilbert for they were grown men at the time and in a position to know “where of they speak.” A

When I last visited Mr. Worley he was 95 years of age—and even after the passage of so many years seemed reluctant to talk of what he knew, but he soon lost his restraint and Mrs. Perry, a resident of the same period who was his housekeeper, verified all statements and clinched the deal with the statement, “I should know, I personally knew one of the men who helped with the lynching.”

Mr. Charles H. Hecht, born in 1882 on the Hecht farm where the hanging took place, says Oldie had two sisters, possibly older and probably not married, but they did live with Red Sylas. There is a disturbing note in the account of Charles H. Hecht, for he states that he positively has seen Red Sylas when he was a small boy and that Sylas continued to live for a time in the community, that he had a large red beard, was a large man, and was drunk each time he saw him.

One story gives an ulterior motive to the whole affair, giving the reason for removing Oldie from the scene as a desire on the part of the Judge to appropriate Oldie's squatter's right on the homestead for his own—which could be. All versions consider Oldie to be innocent of the crime for which he was hanged and all implicate the man who accused him as being the guilty party. It is my opinion that those who were actually involved in the execution of the lynching were victims of misplaced confidence in the word of the accusers.

It is possible that the passage of time pictures Oldie as more nearly innocent than he really was. It would seem there must have been some provocation for good and true men to have gone to the extremes to which they went—and the bystander is always in sympathy with the victim. On the other hand it seems scarcely possible that a nineteen year old boy could have driven stolen horses up from Oregon without the assistance of other men on horseback, and the fact that Oldie had spent that spring working for Charles F. Hecht, the pioneer settler on whose land the hanging took place, makes serious involvement in the horse stealing ring impossible at least for the season of 1882. It is probable that the horses were stolen and quite possible that Oldie knew of this, but since he had remained in the immediately area for a number of months immediately preceding his death, it seems scarcely possible that he could have personally been involved in the illicit purloining of horseflesh.

We cannot know and we should not judge. It was a sordid and regrettable affair at best and it not chronicled as a blot on the history of the community nor on the memory of the uneducated and for the most part unknown participants, but as an exciting event in the typical rough and ready early day existance in a pioneer community. Other such incidents took place in other pioneer communities as the American west grew and matured.

*Herbert Stevens*
*Worley, Idaho*

*Publisher's note: This manuscript was written by Mr. Stevens in 1952, now 23 years back in the past. All the participants in the affair have now been removed by time, and all those persons who could have any personal knowledge of the death of Oldie Neil, with the exception of Mr. Charles H. Hecht, who was only a baby at the time, but who heard the story of Oldie Neil many times described by men who were living in the area in 1882, including of course, his own father, Charles F. Hecht, a pioneer of 1877.*

In 1989 J. Eid of Tualtin, Oregon, wrote a paperback book with the title, THE LYNCHING OF ALDY NEIL, printed by the Bent Tree Press of Tualatin. In 1992 a revised edition was published. Norma Eid states that Aldy's father and her great-grandfather were brothers, certainly she dug into old court records and various sources not available to Herbert Stevens, who wrote his account almost entirely from hearsay. The chief difference in the Eid and Stevens account are in spelling of the name. Stevens gives this as Oldie, and Eid as Aldy (a possible shortening of the name Allday). In the dating, Stevens gives a Sunday in June of 1882, where Eid gives the night of May 21-22 of 1882. Stevens describes the victim as a 19-year-old boy where Eid gives an age of 32 or more. Legends claim that Oldie was innocent, certainly he was never convicted of any crime, but it is improbable that he was completely innocent as in 1881 and 1882 Oldie Neil was accused of horse stealing in court at Cheney, Washington Territory. It is noted that Stevens gives the name of Mike Hawthorne as sheriff but contemporary records say "Sheriff Hatten."

# VIGILANTES RIDE IN 1882

Despite the statement by Henry Desgranges that no confession ever was printed pertaining to the unfortunate hanging of the young man whose story appears on these pages, it would seem that such a confession was printed in the Rockford *Enterprise* in March of 1898. To support this Marjorie Cross very kindly loaned me a copy of the Fairfield *Standard* for March 25, 1898, in which an article appears under the heading, HE HELPED LYNCH ALDY NEAL. *Samuel F. Starr Confesses his Part in that Disgraceful Affair.*

*The Rockford Enterprise last week publishes [sic] a startling confession from Samuel F. Starr, a former resident of Rock Creek valley, but who now lives in Los Angeles, California. Starr confesses to having been implicated in the lynching of Aldy Neal, an alleged horse thief, about seventeen years ago.*

*That horrible incident is still fresh in the minds of the early settlers of this country. W. C. Belknap, who a few years ago cut quite a conspicuous figure in local politics, had employed Neal as a herder. Before and during this time the settlers had lost quite a number of horses and they finally became desperate and decided to make an object lesson of someone. Neal, being very unpopular in the neighborhood, was picked out as a fitting man to take the most important part in the neck-tie party that was suggested. He was captured on what is now the Rose farm, south of the Bethel church. Neal pleaded his innocence and asked for an opportunity to prove the truthfulness of his claims. He was promised a trial, and a posse started to take him to Cheney, then the county seat, when he was overtaken by another mob and lynched to a tree about one and one half miles south-east of Rockford.*

*Later developments established the fact that Neal was innocent of the crime and was a man of good family.*

*About twenty of the early settlers were implicated in the affair, but most of them have moved away and a number have since died.*

The Herbert Stevens manuscript was written in 1952 and a little more knowledge has come to light on the sensitive matter of the printed confession of Samuel F. Starr. It is now believed that only the first installment of the confession was printed in the newspaper. Mr. Desgranges later told Mr. Stevens that he had a signed confession in his possession, however after Mr. Desgranges' death no such confession was found among his personal effects. There have been two views of why Mr. Desgranges did not in the spring of 1898 complete publication of the confession or confessions in his possession, one view was that he was intimidated and the other that his silence had been bought. Mr. Stevens knew Mr. Desgranges personally and feels that neither view has any basis in fact, that Desgranges was a man of courage and integrity and the decision to go no further into the matter was based on the belief that it would do the community no good to further publicize the unfortunate hanging of Oldie Neal, and there were still men living who had taken part in the affair. The decision made by young Editor Desgranges back in March of 1898 is now more than 77 years back in the dusty past and the decision was apparently made in complete sincerity. It should be mentioned also that Samuel F. Starr was a man respected in the community and a public road in Rock Creek valley, southern Spokane county, is named for him. It appears that he wrote out the confession of his own volition, which would take a certain measure of personal integrity. Samuel F. Starr, like Henry Desgranges, seems to have been a pretty good sort of man. These comments are written by the publisher and were not in the Herbert Stevens manuscript, which carefully avoids mentioning the names of respectable citizens who took part in the affair in 1882, now 93 years back in the past.

It is interesting that this account states that horses were stolen in the Rock Creek valley area, which contradicts the probably correct version that while Oldie Neal was guarding stolen horses at the time of his capture, it is assumed that these were not animals taken from local residents.

This same issue of the Fairfield *Standard* carries an account of the wedding of Thomas D. Hench and Miss Marguerite E. Dashiell, the parents of Mrs. R. B.( Marjorie) Cross. We note that Pierce Green had a house and lots for sale in Fairfield for a price of five hundred dollars. The Fairfield Meat Market, A. Anderson, Proprietor, offered to buy cattle, hogs, and poultry. The Fairfield Planing Mill, owned by Alex Nastes, offered moulding, stair-railing, ballusters, and newel posts. The Bank of Latah, B. F. O'Neill, banker, advertised its services. The Coey Mercantile Company advertised Canton plows, Superior drills, the Clipper fanning mill, and the "Boss" washing machine. C. A. Loy & Co., also of Fairfield, advertised a carload of nails just received, a full line of doors and windows, a new invoice of mixed paints, a carload of coal, plow single trees, Glidden barbed wire, and the renowned "Western" washer. E. S. Burgan & Co. of Latah, advertised 20 pounds of bluestone for 1.00, or for the same price 25 yards of good calico or 15 pounds of granulated sugar. And referring rather delicately to the weather we find this item: A four inch fall of the beautiful this morning has put a stop to farm work for about a week.

*Glen Adams, publisher*

SMLuke